The REVOLUTION
IN INDUSTRY

JOHN PERRITANO

Crabtree Publishing Company
www.crabtreebooks.com

Crabtree Publishing Company

www.crabtreebooks.com

Author:
John Perritano
Coordinating editor:
Chester Fisher
Editors:
Scholastic Ventures Inc.
Molly Aloian
Copy editor:
Scholastic Ventures Inc.
Proofreaders:
Adrianna Morganelli
Crystal Sikkens
Project editor:
Robert Walker
Production coordinator:
Katherine Kantor

Prepress technicians:
Ken Wright
Katherine Kantor
Logo design:
Samantha Crabtree
Project manager:
Santosh Vasudevan (Q2AMedia)
Art direction:
Rahul Dhiman (Q2AMedia)
Design:
Tarang Saggar (Q2AMedia)
Illustrations:
Q2AMedia

Library and Archives Canada Cataloguing in Publication

Perritano, John
  The revolution in industry / John Perritano.

(Graphic America)
Includes index.
ISBN 978-0-7787-4189-3 (bound).--ISBN 978-0-7787-4216-6 (pbk.)

  1. Technological innovations--Comic books, strips, etc.--
Juvenile literature. 2. Industrialization--Comic books, strips,
etc.--Juvenile literature. I. Title. II. Series.

T173.8.P47 2008   j609   C2008-906283-3

Library of Congress Cataloging-in-Publication Data

Perritano, John.
  The revolution in industry / John Perritano.
    p. cm. -- (Graphic America)
  Includes index.
  ISBN-13: 978-0-7787-4216-6 (pbk. : alk. paper)
  ISBN-10: 0-7787-4216-4 (pbk. : alk. paper)
  ISBN-13: 978-0-7787-4189-3 (reinforced library binding : alk. paper)
  ISBN-10: 0-7787-4189-3 (reinforced library binding : alk. paper)
  1. Technological innovations--Juvenile literature. 2.
Industrialization--Juvenile literature. I. Title. II. Series.

  T173.8.K47 1990
  609--dc22
                                        2008041855

Crabtree Publishing Company

www.crabtreebooks.com   1-800-387-7650

**Published
in Canada
Crabtree Publishing**
616 Welland Ave.
St. Catharines, ON
L2M 5V6

**Published in the
United States
Crabtree Publishing**
PMB16A
350 Fifth Ave., Suite 3308
New York, NY 10118

**Published in the
United Kingdom
Crabtree Publishing**
White Cross Mills
High Town, Lancaster
LA1 4XS

**Published in
Australia
Crabtree Publishing**
386 Mt. Alexander Rd.
Ascot Vale (Melbourne)
VIC 3032

CONTENTS

QUEST FOR POWER

PEOPLE HAVE ALWAYS SEARCHED FOR BETTER WAYS TO USE MACHINES. THIS QUEST FOR POWER HAS LED THEM TO BUILD HUGE SHIPS THAT CAN TRAVEL ACROSS THE OCEANS...

AND AIRPLANES THAT FLY THROUGH THE AIR...

AND VEHICLES THAT MOTOR DOWN PAVED HIGHWAYS.

THEY HAVE ALSO BUILT SUBMARINES THAT GET THEIR ENERGY FROM NUCLEAR POWER...

AND SPACE STATIONS POWERED BY ENERGY FROM THE SUN.

PEOPLE POWER

LONG AGO, PEOPLE DEPENDED ONLY ON THEIR BODIES TO **GENERATE** POWER. THEY CARVED BOATS FROM TREES AND USED THEIR MUSCLES TO ROW DOWN RIVERS AND ACROSS LAKES.

FARMERS DUG UP FIELDS BY HAND.

ANIMAL POWER

PEOPLE BEGAN TO REALIZE THAT ANIMALS WERE GOOD SOURCES OF POWER. OXEN PULLED PLOWS TO HELP DIG THE HEAVY SOIL.

MULES TURNED STONES THAT CRUSHED GRAIN INTO FLOUR.

HORSES ALLOWED PEOPLE TO TRAVEL FROM PLACE TO PLACE.

WIND POWER

THE WIND PROVIDED LOTS OF POWER, TOO. EARLY **IMMIGRANTS** TO AMERICA FROM THE NETHERLANDS BUILT WINDMILLS TO GRIND GRAIN.

WIND MOVED MIGHTY SHIPS ACROSS VAST OCEANS.

WATER POWER

RUSHING WATER TURNED SAW BLADES THAT CUT TREES INTO BOARDS.

WATER ALSO POWERED CARTING MILLS THAT TURNED FLEECE INTO THREAD.

THE STEAM ENGINE

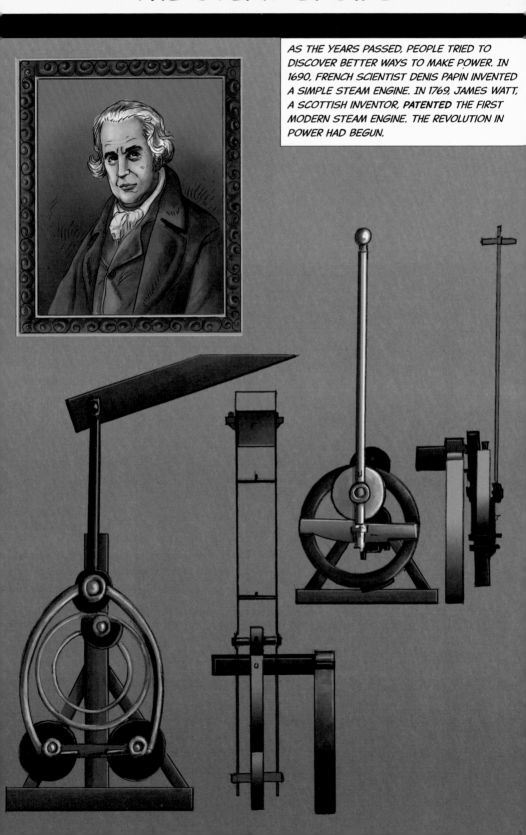

AS THE YEARS PASSED, PEOPLE TRIED TO DISCOVER BETTER WAYS TO MAKE POWER. IN 1690, FRENCH SCIENTIST DENIS PAPIN INVENTED A SIMPLE STEAM ENGINE. IN 1769, JAMES WATT, A SCOTTISH INVENTOR, **PATENTED** THE FIRST MODERN STEAM ENGINE. THE REVOLUTION IN POWER HAD BEGUN.

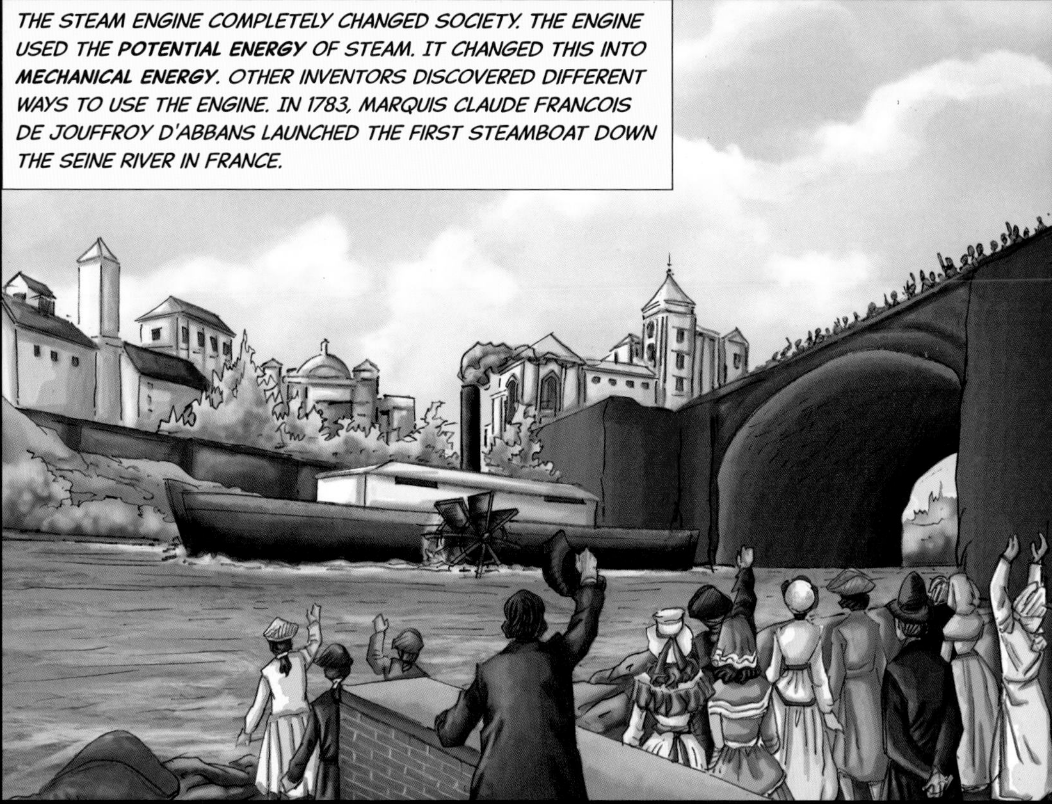
THE STEAM ENGINE COMPLETELY CHANGED SOCIETY. THE ENGINE USED THE **POTENTIAL ENERGY** OF STEAM. IT CHANGED THIS INTO **MECHANICAL ENERGY**. OTHER INVENTORS DISCOVERED DIFFERENT WAYS TO USE THE ENGINE. IN 1783, MARQUIS CLAUDE FRANCOIS DE JOUFFROY D'ABBANS LAUNCHED THE FIRST STEAMBOAT DOWN THE SEINE RIVER IN FRANCE.

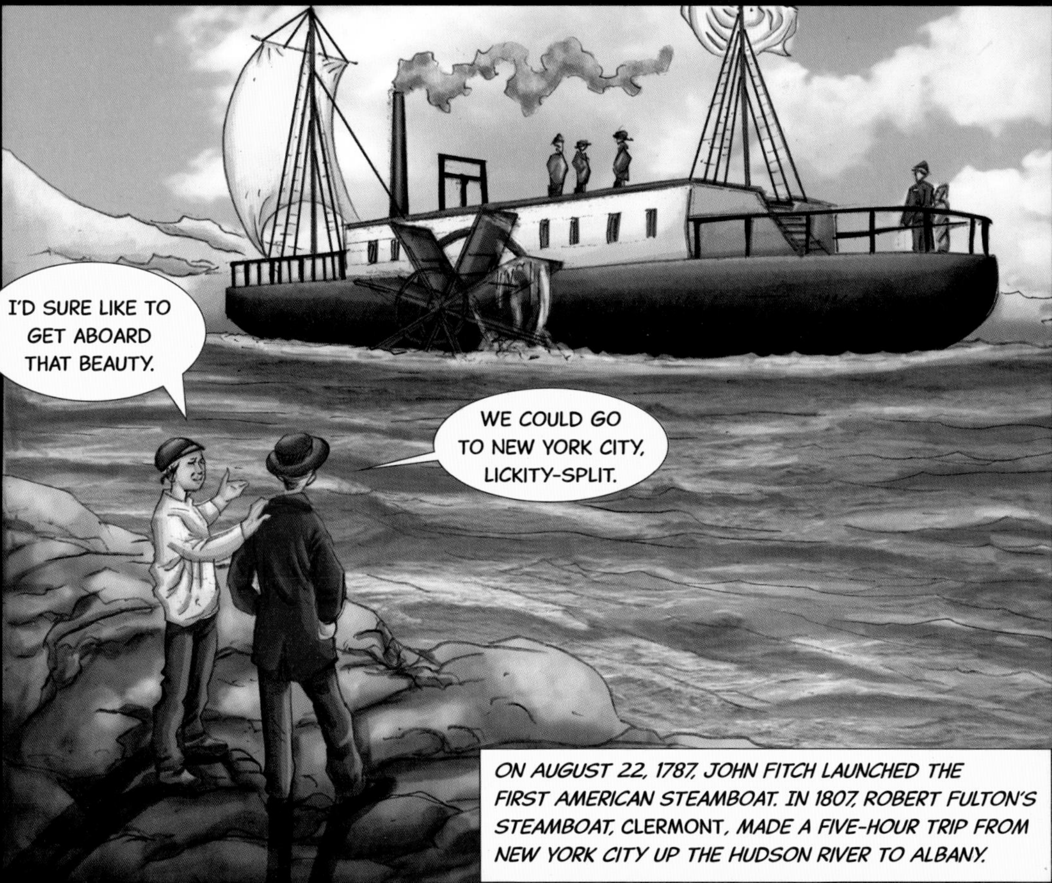
I'D SURE LIKE TO GET ABOARD THAT BEAUTY.
WE COULD GO TO NEW YORK CITY, LICKITY-SPLIT.
ON AUGUST 22, 1787, JOHN FITCH LAUNCHED THE FIRST AMERICAN STEAMBOAT. IN 1807, ROBERT FULTON'S STEAMBOAT, CLERMONT, MADE A FIVE-HOUR TRIP FROM NEW YORK CITY UP THE HUDSON RIVER TO ALBANY.

STEAM TRAINS

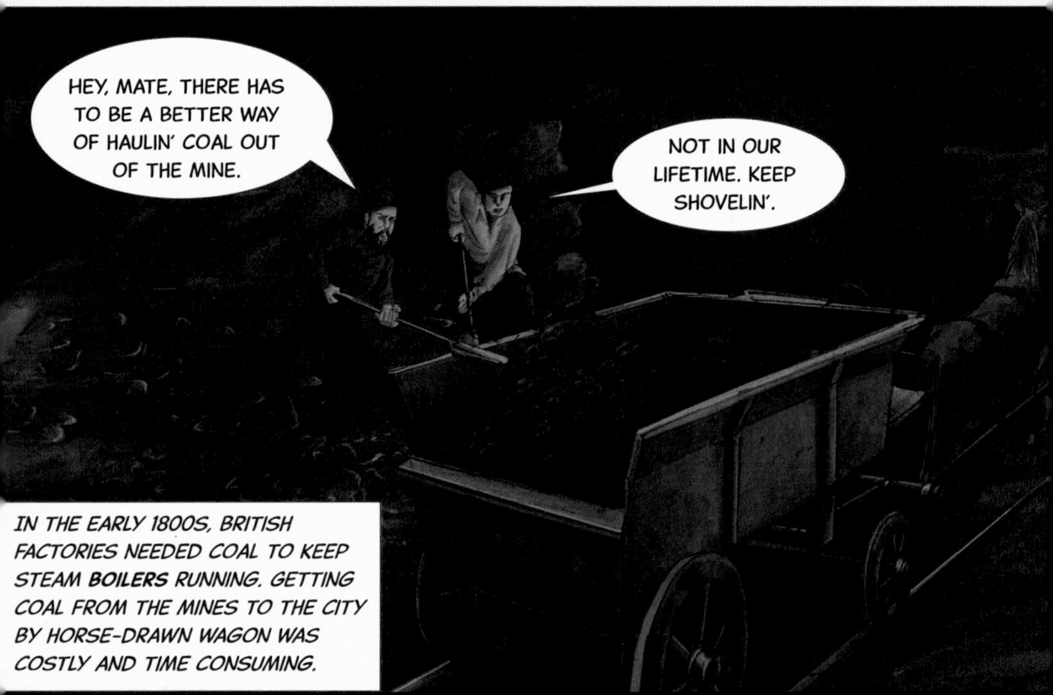
HEY, MATE, THERE HAS TO BE A BETTER WAY OF HAULIN' COAL OUT OF THE MINE.
NOT IN OUR LIFETIME. KEEP SHOVELIN'.
IN THE EARLY 1800S, BRITISH FACTORIES NEEDED COAL TO KEEP STEAM **BOILERS** RUNNING. GETTING COAL FROM THE MINES TO THE CITY BY HORSE-DRAWN WAGON WAS COSTLY AND TIME CONSUMING.

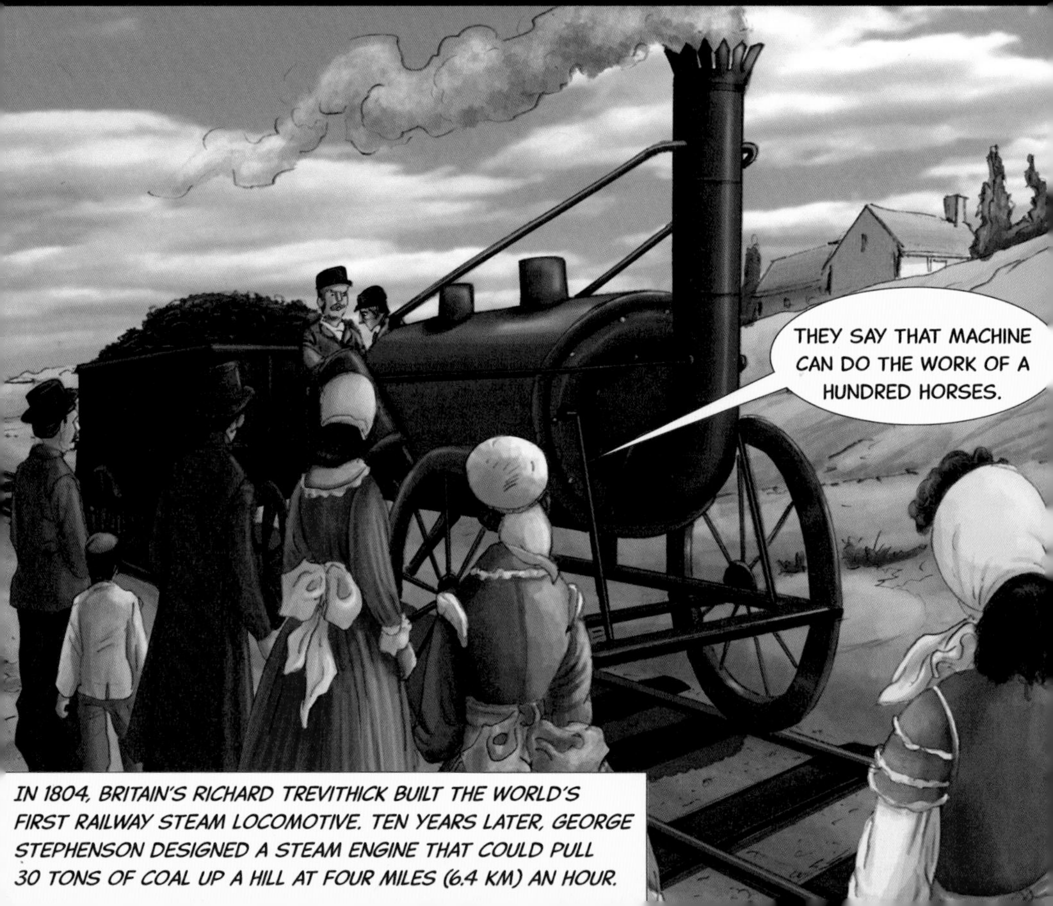
THEY SAY THAT MACHINE CAN DO THE WORK OF A HUNDRED HORSES.
IN 1804, BRITAIN'S RICHARD TREVITHICK BUILT THE WORLD'S FIRST RAILWAY STEAM LOCOMOTIVE. TEN YEARS LATER, GEORGE STEPHENSON DESIGNED A STEAM ENGINE THAT COULD PULL 30 TONS OF COAL UP A HILL AT FOUR MILES (6.4 KM) AN HOUR.

IT WAS NOT LONG BEFORE STEAM TRAINS STARTED MOVING BOTH **FREIGHT** AND PEOPLE. TOWNS QUICKLY GREW ALONG RAILROAD STOPS. THE RAILROAD COMPANIES CREATED THOUSANDS OF JOBS. BUSINESSES IN TOWNS ALONG A TRAIN'S ROUTE NEEDED WORKERS. THE RAILROAD NEEDED PEOPLE TO MOVE FREIGHT ON AND OFF TRAINS. FACTORIES HIRED MORE WORKERS TO HELP MEET THE DEMAND WHEN ITEMS SOLD AROUND THE COUNTRY.

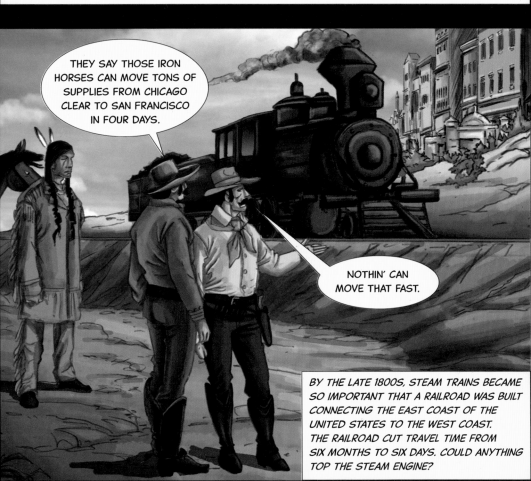

BY THE LATE 1800S, STEAM TRAINS BECAME SO IMPORTANT THAT A RAILROAD WAS BUILT CONNECTING THE EAST COAST OF THE UNITED STATES TO THE WEST COAST. THE RAILROAD CUT TRAVEL TIME FROM SIX MONTHS TO SIX DAYS. COULD ANYTHING TOP THE STEAM ENGINE?

THE INTERNAL COMBUSTION ENGINE

THE INTERNAL COMBUSTION ENGINE SOON MADE THE STEAM ENGINE SEEM LIKE A TOY. INSTEAD OF HEATING WATER TO MAKE STEAM, THE INTERNAL COMBUSTION ENGINE USED A SMALL AMOUNT OF EXPLODING FUEL TO CREATE ENERGY.

I'M CONFIDENT THAT THIS ENGINE WILL HELP MAKE THE WORLD A BETTER PLACE.

MANY INVENTORS TRIED TO FIND WAYS OF USING THE NEW ENGINE TO POWER MACHINES. NIKOLAUS OTTO INVENTED ONE OF THE FIRST GASOLINE-POWERED ENGINES.

THE AUTOMOBILE

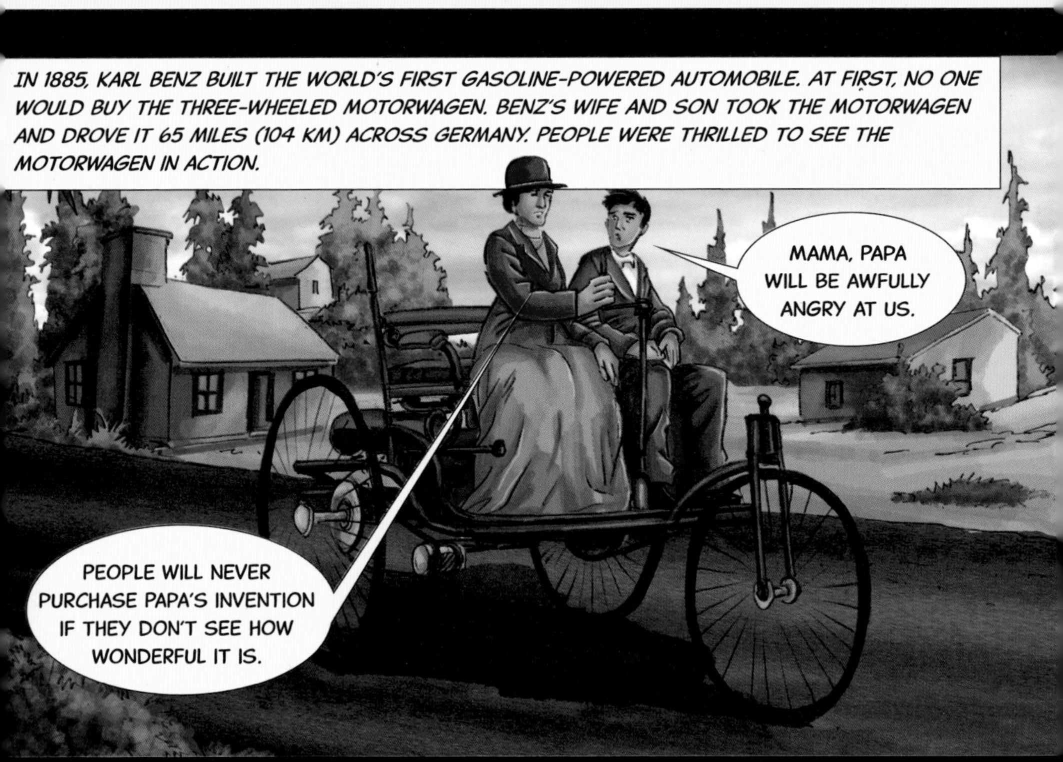
IN 1885, KARL BENZ BUILT THE WORLD'S FIRST GASOLINE-POWERED AUTOMOBILE. AT FIRST, NO ONE WOULD BUY THE THREE-WHEELED MOTORWAGEN. BENZ'S WIFE AND SON TOOK THE MOTORWAGEN AND DROVE IT 65 MILES (104 KM) ACROSS GERMANY. PEOPLE WERE THRILLED TO SEE THE MOTORWAGEN IN ACTION.
MAMA, PAPA WILL BE AWFULLY ANGRY AT US.
PEOPLE WILL NEVER PURCHASE PAPA'S INVENTION IF THEY DON'T SEE HOW WONDERFUL IT IS.

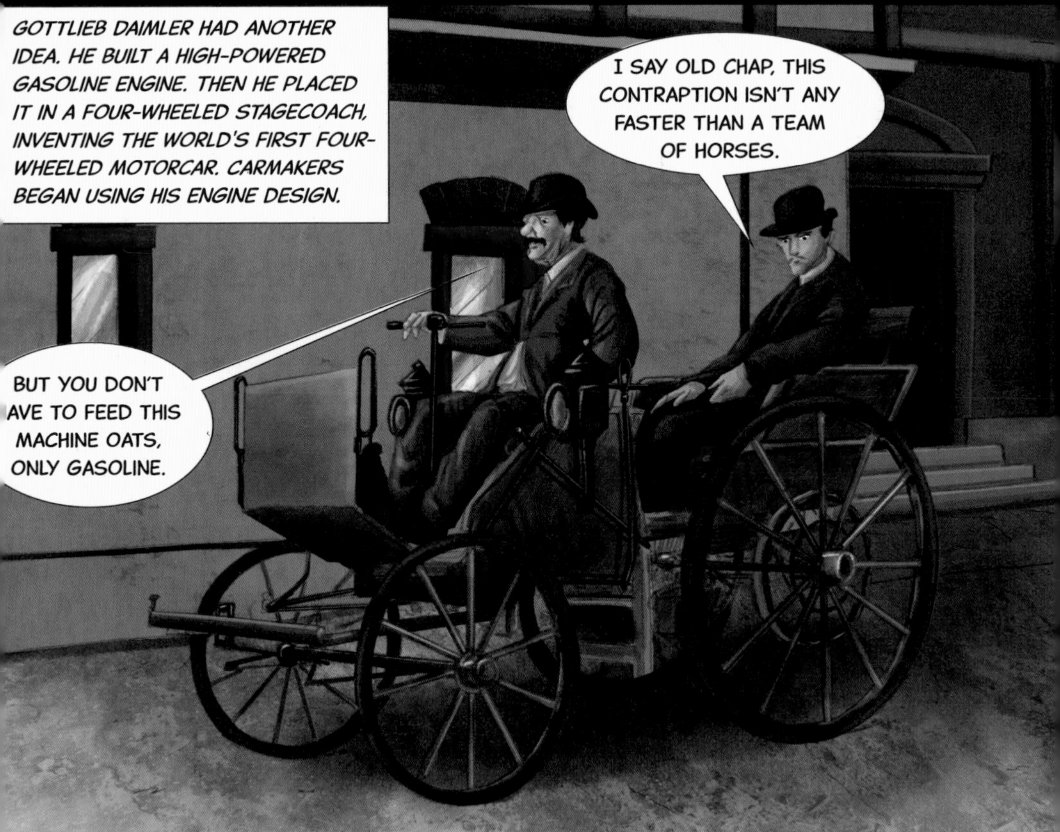
GOTTLIEB DAIMLER HAD ANOTHER IDEA. HE BUILT A HIGH-POWERED GASOLINE ENGINE. THEN HE PLACED IT IN A FOUR-WHEELED STAGECOACH, INVENTING THE WORLD'S FIRST FOUR-WHEELED MOTORCAR. CARMAKERS BEGAN USING HIS ENGINE DESIGN.
I SAY OLD CHAP, THIS CONTRAPTION ISN'T ANY FASTER THAN A TEAM OF HORSES.
BUT YOU DON'T AVE TO FEED THIS MACHINE OATS, ONLY GASOLINE.

THE WRIGHT STUFF

THE INTERNAL COMBUSTION ENGINE IMPACTED PEOPLE'S LIVES IN MANY WAYS. YET, IT TOOK TWO BROTHERS FROM DAYTON, OHIO—ORVILLE AND WILBUR WRIGHT—TO TAKE THE ENGINE TO NEW HEIGHTS. THEY USED IT TO BUILD THE FIRST MECHANICALLY POWERED AIRPLANE.

DECEMBER 17, 1903, WAS A COOL AND WINDY DAY ON THE REMOTE ISLAND OF KITTY HAWK, NORTH CAROLINA. AT 10:35 A.M., ORVILLE WRIGHT CLIMBED ABOARD A STRANGE-LOOKING MACHINE WITH WINGS. THE GASOLINE-POWERED ENGINE TURNED THE MACHINE'S TWO PROPELLERS.

EVERYTHING CHECKS OUT, ORVILLE. GOOD LUCK TO YOU.

WITH THE PROPELLERS SPINNING AND WILBUR RUNNING ALONG SIDE, THE MACHINE WENT DOWN A WOODEN RAIL AT SEVEN MILES (11 KM) PER HOUR. AS THE AIRPLANE LUMBERED ALONG THE SKIDS, IT BEGAN TO RISE SLOWLY.

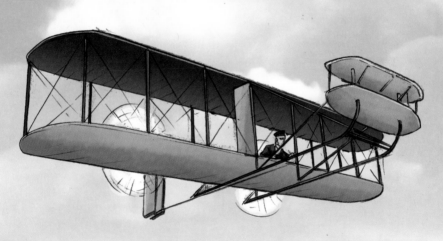

ONLY MOMENTS LATER, THE AIRPLANE ROSE TO A HEIGHT OF ABOUT 10 FEET (THREE METERS). IT FLEW FOR AN AMAZING 120 FEET (37 M). ORVILLE WRIGHT HAD BECOME THE FIRST PERSON TO FLY A MOTORIZED AIRCRAFT.

SOARING HIGHER

THE WRIGHT BROTHERS' FLIGHT LASTED ONLY 12 SECONDS, BUT IT CHANGED THE WORLD. **ENGINEERS** SOON MADE THE WRIGHT BROTHERS' INVENTION SLEEKER, FASTER, AND LARGER. THIS AMAZING INVENTION WAS FIRST USED DURING WORLD WAR I (1914-1918). FRANCE, GERMANY, GREAT BRITAIN, AND THE UNITED STATES USED THE AIRPLANES AS A WEAPON FOR THE FIRST TIME. GUNS WERE MOUNTED ON AIRPLANES, AND FIGHTING TOOK TO THE SKIES.

PROPELLER AIRPLANES GAVE WAY TO THE *JET* BY THE 1940S. JET ENGINES MADE AIRPLANES FLY FASTER THAN THE SPEED OF SOUND, ABOUT 700 MILES (1127 KM) AN HOUR. CAPTAIN CHARLES "CHUCK" YEAGER WAS THE FIRST TO BREAK THE SOUND BARRIER ON OCTOBER 14, 1947, IN A JET HE NAMED AFTER HIS WIFE.

ROCKETS AND MORE

BY THE 1950S, ROCKET ENGINES PROVIDED ENOUGH POWER FOR PEOPLE TO ESCAPE EARTH'S GRAVITY. THE SATURN V ROCKET, WHICH SENT PEOPLE TO THE MOON, WAS THE MOST POWERFUL ROCKET EVER BUILT.

"LIFT OFF; WE HAVE A LIFT OFF, 32 MINUTES PAST THE HOUR. LIFT OFF ON APOLLO 11."

THE MAIN ENGINES OF THE SPACE SHUTTLE USE LIQUID HYDROGEN AND OXYGEN AS FUEL. THE ENGINES PROVIDE ENOUGH POWER FOR THE SHUTTLE TO SPEED UP FROM 3,000 MILES PER HOUR (4,828 KM/H) TO 17,000 MILES PER HOUR (27,359 KM/H) IN JUST SIX MINUTES.

NUCLEAR POWER

"NOW, I AM BECOME DEATH, THE DESTROYER OF WORLDS."—DR. J. ROBERT OPPENHEIMER, WHO HELPED DEVELOP THE ATOMIC BOMB.

NO POWER IS AS GREAT AS THE ENERGY CREATED BY A **NUCLEAR REACTION**. SCIENTISTS DISCOVERED THE POWER OF THE ATOM IN 1945. SCIENTISTS UNDERSTOOD THAT IF THEY COULD BREAK APART JUST ONE SMALL ATOM, THE REACTION WOULD RELEASE A GREAT AMOUNT OF ENERGY. THEY SPLIT URANIUM ATOMS TO CREATE A VERY STRONG SOURCE OF POWER.

SCIENTISTS LEARNED HOW TO CONTROL NUCLEAR REACTIONS. THE U.S. NAVY'S *NAUTILUS* WAS THE FIRST NUCLEAR-POWERED SUBMARINE. THE NUCLEAR POWER ALLOWED THE SUBMARINES TO STAY AT SEA LONGER WITHOUT NEEDING TO REFUEL. OLDER SUBMARINES COULD ONLY STAY UNDER WATER FOR A FEW DAYS AT MOST. NUCLEAR SUBMARINES CAN STAY UNDER WATER LONG ENOUGH TO SAIL AROUND THE WORLD DOZENS OF TIMES.

IN 1997, THE UNITED STATES LAUNCHED THE CASSINI *SPACECRAFT* TO SATURN. THE MACHINE USED A SPECIAL ENGINE POWERED BY **PLUTONIUM**. LIKE URANIUM, IT PROVIDES NUCLEAR ENERGY. IT TAKES FAR LESS PLUTONIUM TO POWER A ROCKET THAN ROCKET FUEL.

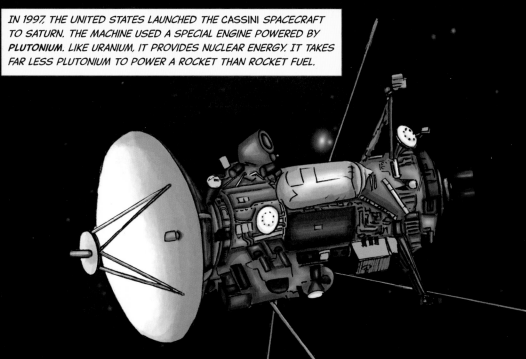

POWERING INTO THE FUTURE

TRAINS USED TO BE LUMBERING GIANTS. A FEW COUNTRIES ARE NOW USING FAST MAGLEV TRAINS. MAGLEV IS SHORT FOR MAGNETIC LEVITATION. USING THE POWER OF **ELECTROMAGNETS**, THE TRAINS FLOAT OVER A TRACK. MAGLEV TRAINS TRAVEL UP TO 310 MILES PER HOUR (499 KM/H).

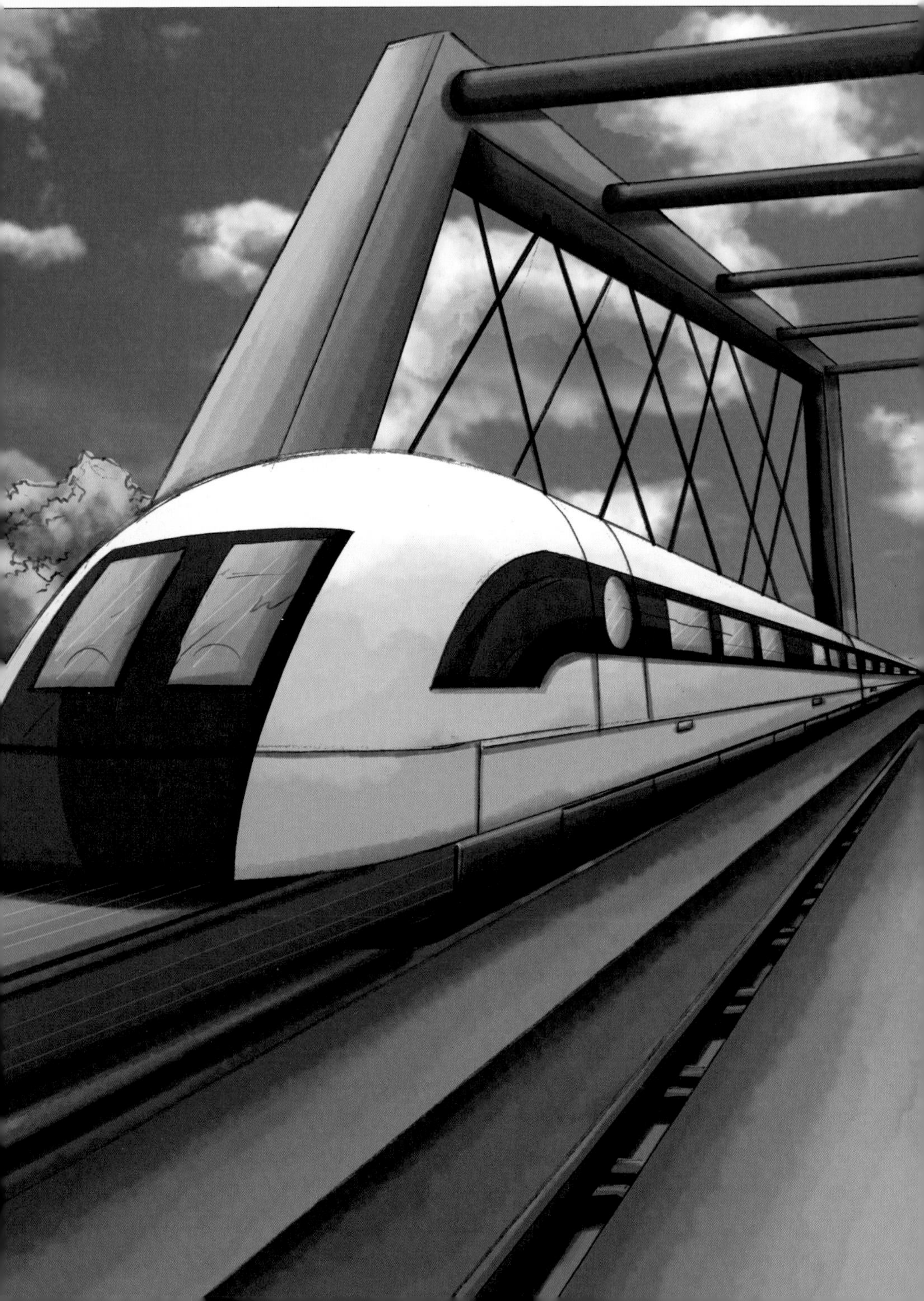

THE REVOLUTION CONTINUES

TIMELINE

1690 — FRENCH SCIENTIST DENIS PAPIN DEVELOPS THE FIRST STEAM ENGINE.

1769 — JAMES WATT FILES FOR A PATENT FOR HIS STEAM ENGINE.

1783 — THE WORLD'S FIRST STEAMBOAT MAKES ITS DEBUT IN FRANCE.

1787 — JOHN FITCH INTRODUCES THE FIRST AMERICAN STEAM BOAT ON THE DELAWARE RIVER NEAR PHILADELPHIA, AS THE DELEGATES TO THE CONSTITUTIONAL CONVENTION LOOK ON.

1804 — RICHARD TREVITHICK BUILDS THE WORLD'S FIRST STEAM LOCOMOTIVE.

1807 — ROBERT FULTON'S FIRST STEAMBOAT, THE CLERMONT, SETS SAIL ON THE HUDSON RIVER FROM NEW YORK CITY TO ALBANY.

1814 — FULTON BEGINS REGULAR STEAMBOAT SERVICE ON THE MISSISSIPPI RIVER.

1869 — THE TRANSCONTINENTAL RAILROAD IS COMPLETED.

1885 — GOTTLIEB DAIMLER INVENTS THE WORLD'S FIRST MOTORCYCLE.

1885 — KARL BENZ BUILDS THE WORLD'S FIRST GASOLINE-POWERED AUTOMOBILE.

1903 — THE WRIGHT BROTHERS' FIRST AIRPLANE TAKES OFF AT KITTY HAWK, NORTH CAROLINA.

1913 — HENRY FORD PUTS THE FIRST ASSEMBLY LINE TO USE.

1945 — THE WORLD'S FIRST ATOMIC BOMB EXPLODES.

1947 — CHUCK YEAGER BECOMES THE FIRST HUMAN TO FLY FASTER THAN THE SPEED OF SOUND.

1954 — THE WORLD'S FIRST NUCLEAR-POWERED SUBMARINE, THE NAUTILUS, SETS SAIL.

1960S — JAPAN BUILDS ITS FIRST MAGLEV TRAIN LINE.

1969 — APOLLO 11 BLASTS OFF FOR THE MOON.

1981 — THE COLUMBIA BECOMES THE FIRST SPACE SHUTTLE TO ORBIT EARTH.

1997 — NASA LAUNCHES CASSINI PROBE TO SATURN.

GLOSSARY

ASSEMBLY LINE A METHOD OF MASS PRODUCTION DURING WHICH A PRODUCT, SUCH AS AN AUTOMOBILE, IS BUILT STEP BY STEP BY DIFFERENT WORKERS ADDING ONE PART AT A TIME

BOILERS A VESSEL THAT CONVERTS WATER INTO STEAM WHICH DRIVE ELECTRICAL GENERATORS

ELECTROMAGNET A TYPE OF MAGNET IN WHICH AN ELECTRICAL CURRENT PRODUCES A MAGNETIC FIELD

ENGINEER A PERSON WHO USES SCIENCE TO DESIGN MACHINES, ROADS, RAILWAYS, BRIDGES, SHIPS, AND OTHER THINGS

FREIGHT GOODS CARRIED BY A VESSEL OR A VEHICLE

GENERATE TO PRODUCE; TO CREATE

IMMIGRANT A PERSON WHO LEAVES ONE'S OWN COUNTRY TO SETTLE IN A NEW PLACE

JET A TYPE OF AIRPLANE THAT MOVES RAPIDLY THROUGH AIR IN ONE DIRECTION, PROPELLED BY A STREAM OF GASES MOVING IN THE OTHER

MECHANICAL ENERGY THE ENERGY OF AN OBJECT DUE TO ITS MOTION

NUCLEAR POWER ENERGY THAT COMES FROM A NUCLEAR REACTION

NUCLEAR REACTION CHANGES INVOLVING ATOMS

PATENT A DOCUMENT THAT PREVENTS OTHER PEOPLE FROM COPYING AN INVENTOR'S IDEA FOR A CERTAIN PERIOD OF TIME

PLUTONIUM AN ELEMENT USED IN NUCLEAR MATERIAL

POTENTIAL ENERGY STORED ENERGY; POTENTIAL ENERGY CAN BE RELEASED AND CONVERTED INTO OTHER TYPES OF ENERGY

INDEX

WEBFINDER

HTTP://WWW.THEHENRYFORD.ORG/EXHIBITS/HF/

HTTP://XROADS.VIRGINIA.EDU/~HYPER/DETOC/TRANSPORT/FULTON.HTML

HTTP://WWW.AECL.CA/KIDSZONE/ATOMICENERGY/NUCLEAR/INDEX.ASP

HTTP://WWW.GRC.NASA.GOV/WWW/WRIGHT/INDEX.HTM

HTTP://WWW.MOLLER.COM/

PRINTED IN THE U.S.A. - BG